A Journey
For Felix

Janice M Lovato

☺ *Little kids can now read along!*
Just look for the happy face and take the journey with Felix!

A Journey for Felix by Janice Lovato
Illustrated by Justin T. Lovato

Felix watched Germaine and his father walk away. Then he happily turned back and looked at his own family. He was so glad that he finally found them and he was happy that Germaine had found his father also. He smiled and could hardly wait until he was in a safe home where he and his family would be protected.

They traveled up a hill that was a bit steep. The hot sun wasn't making the journey any easier and Felix knew that his family would need to find a safe place for the night.

Felix suggested to his father that they start to think of a place to set up camp before it got dark. Felix's father agreed and picked a spot. His mother started looking for food and his little brother Tommy started preparing for bed.

Felix watched Germaine and his father walk away Felix was happy he found his family. Now that they were together they could start the journey to their new home.

Felix was hungry however, he knew that he needed to help his father gather materials to make a camp. Felix's mother gathered some leaves and grass for them to eat. Felix was happy that he could sleep without worrying about anything. His father was there now and he was always the one to protect the family.

Felix notices the sky getting dark. He tells his father it is time to look for a place to camp. They stop and his little brother Tommy falls asleep, but Felix is too hungry to sleep. He helps his father set up camp and gets a good meal and lies down.

Felix woke the next morning, climbed up out of the hole and could not find his family. Felix looked around and called to his family. He scanned the whole area but there was no sign of them. Felix soon began to realize that he was all alone. He could not figure out where his family was. He looked all around and called out to them but they were nowhere to be found. Felix started to worry that something had happened to them. He kept looking but was losing hope as he looked. He did not know what to do.

He sat on the ground with tears in his eyes and looked up at the sky. He had to find out what happened to them and he was determined to do so. Felix gathered what he needed to survive and started walking. He came upon a stream where he could cool off, and maybe find more food. He kept looking in the water at his reflection. He saw a sad beetle that didn't have any hope in the world.

☺ *Felix sleeps really well that night. He is safe and is not afraid of anything. He wakes up to have breakfast the next morning but his family is not there. He cannot find them anywhere.*

He picked himself up from the water and started to walk towards a hill. He walked a long time before he came upon a park where there were picnic benches and people in the park. He watched the children run and play ball and the adults sitting in chairs eating snacks and drinking soda. Felix made his way over to a chair and stayed underneath it.

Felix knows he is all alone and he is very sad, but he cannot give up. He starts his journey to find his family.

Felix was hungry and tired so he figured the shade would be a great place to rest. All the children looked like they were having a lot of fun and Felix began to remember when he did not have a worry in the world. Felix wasn't prepared to take care of himself but he knew he could if he had to. He learned a lot from Germaine. Felix found a piece of cloth hanging from the chair he was underneath. He covered himself with the cloth and made a little bed then soon fell asleep.

He comes to a park where he can see children playing. He can also see their parents sitting in chairs watching them. Felix sneaks underneath one of the chairs and falls asleep.

He slept for a while but was rudely awakened when he was thrown from the piece of cloth. He tried to escape but got trapped between a red plastic box and a wall. Felix did not know what to do. All he could hear was a bunch of talking and laughing. Then he heard the sound of closing doors and a vibrating sound. Felix tried to relax because he knew there was nothing he could do to get out of the situation.

Suddenly the vibrating stopped and Felix could hear the doors opening and the sound of kids running and playing. Soon he could feel himself being moved and put down. He was in the dark and he did not know what to do. The cloth fell on top of him and began to suffocate. Felix struggled to get free. Then two little girls showed up in the barn.

When he wakes up he is trapped in a car. Scared he does not know where he is going. All he knows is that it is far away from his family.

One of the girls saw Felix and screamed as she pointed at him. He knew his life was over and that there was no way to get out of this situation. The little girl told her friend not to harm him.

He did not make it very far because the family dog discovered him and started to go after him. Felix did his best to hide from the dog. He was so nervous that his heart was beating so hard he could feel it moving his entire body. He grabbed on to a piece of wood and ran under it as fast as he could when he felt a wet sensation and warm air coming his way.

He finds himself in a dark barn. A young girl screams when she sees him. The other girl that is with her tries to save his life.

The dog was sniffing around for Felix but could not find him. All Felix could see was a moist dark brown nose coming his way, and he was either going to be discovered and eaten or lucky enough not to be seen. As the dog's wet nose got closer to him, he started to close his eyes and flinch. Felix was so scared he did not know what to do, when suddenly the little girl called the dog over to her.

She picks him up and holds him in her hands when the family dog discovers him. She walks to the table and shows the young girl that he is helpless.

She picked up Felix and yelled at the dog. Felix decided to relax again. She put him back on the ground. He watched the girls as they played in the barn and wondered where his family could be and if he would ever see them again. He felt alone. It began to get dark outside and the barn turned pitch black.

The other little girl shrugged her shoulders, but decided not to kill him. When she lays him down on the soft hay he is thankful and says a prayer for his family. Then he looks up at the huge barn he is in and wonders what will happen. next?

After just a few hours, Felix heard some scratching towards the back of the barn. He looked up and he could see a little shadow but could not make out what it was. He got closer and realized it was a gopher looking for either a warm bed or a nice meal. Felix knew he would be the meal if he did not get out of there quickly. He tried hiding under hay but the gopher kept searching through it. Felix decided to climb up a shovel to get to the top and hide from the gopher. He watched from the top of the handle as the gopher kept digging.

While resting on the hay he starts to feel lonely. Then suddenly he was discovered by a gopher. The gopher starts coming after Felix so he runs up a shovel handle.

Felix stayed on the shovel handle but did not know how long he would last up there. As he watched from where he was, he could see that the gopher was not giving up. Suddenly he saw a huge web with an albino spider and all he could think about was how he was going to get out of the situation.

The spider was huge and very scary looking. It was white and had dark brown stripes on it. He could see the spider's fangs dripping with mucus and its black shiny eyes observing him. The spider's long skinny hairy legs started moving towards him. Felix prayed that it could not see him because he was going to be dinner for either the gopher or the spider and he did not want to be either. He wanted to run away but did not have many options as to where he could go.

While hiding from the gopher on the shovel handle, he is discovered by a very hungry Albino spider. Felix starts to panic.

He backed up so the spider could not see him but lost his footing on the shovel handle. He felt his little body slipping off the handle and the one leg still holding on was shaking so bad he knew he was going to fall no matter what he did. He scrambled to catch any foot holds he could but kept slipping no matter what he tried. With whatever energy he had left, he grabbed on to the tip of the shovel handle and barely pulled himself to safety. When he got back to the top the spider was waiting for him. Just then, the spider spotted a fly that had gotten caught in its web and decided to forget about Felix and have a snack.

Felix took his chance to get away from the spider and ran down the shovel handle. Felix found a little hole in the side of the barn wall and hid in there. His heart was beating really fast and he was not able to think.

The spider starts to come after him. He loses his footing and starts to fall. Hanging by a leg he feels his life is over. He uses all his strength and pulls himself up. He barley gets away and finds a hole in the wall and falls asleep.

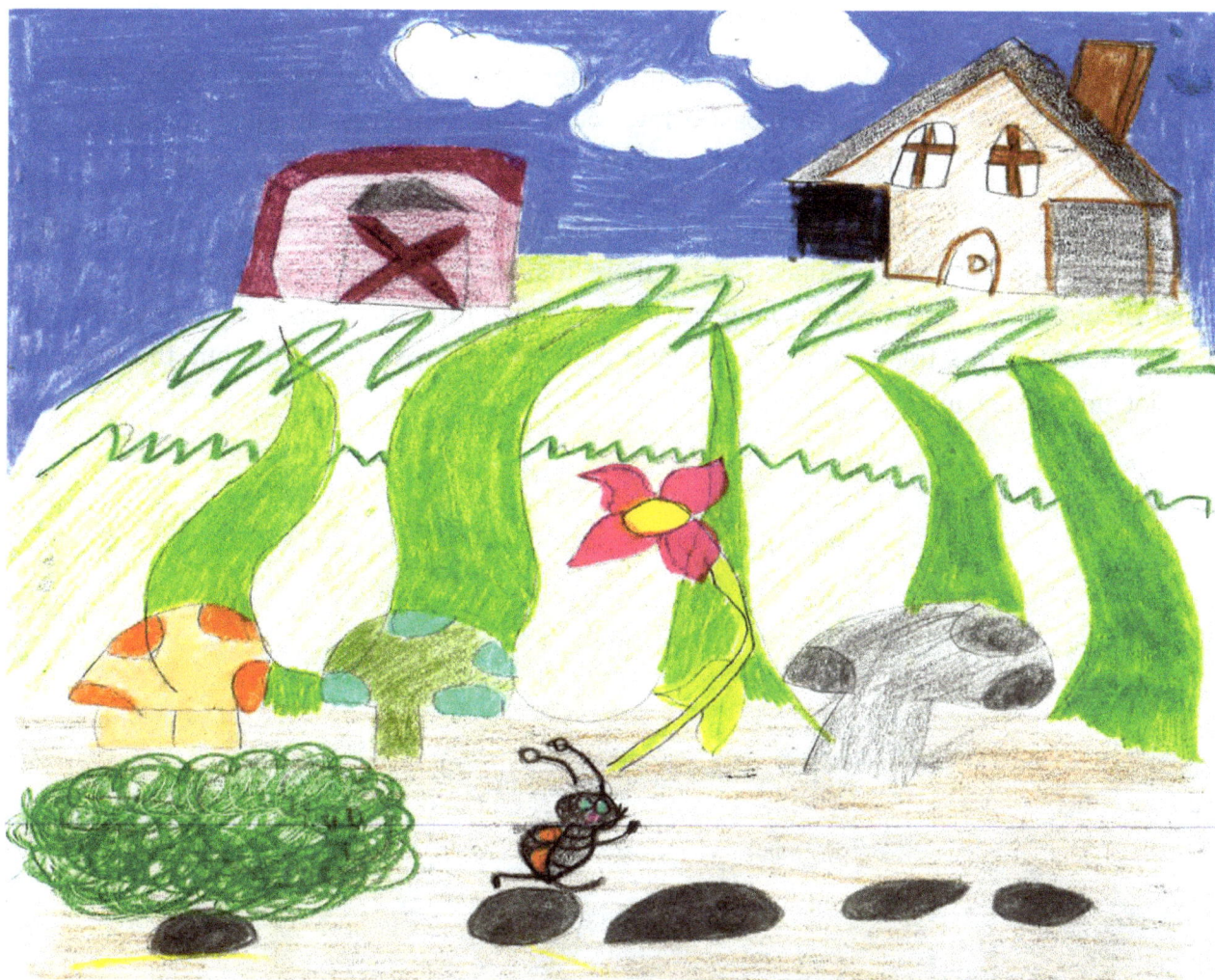

The next morning Felix jumped up and bumped his head when he heard the rooster crow. He fell back down and suddenly remembered where he was.

He jumped down off the barn wall and started to plan his day. Since he knew the dog and gopher would probably be around he had to be careful. He looked out of the barn and saw acres and acres of grass. The sprinklers were watering the grass and the grass was very green. Wow! He thought of all the food that grass would provide.

🙂 *The next morning he wakes up and starts his journey. He sees tall blades of grass dripping with water from the sprinklers. Everything is nice and fresh.*

Once the sprinklers stopped he waited for the water to settle on the ground before he went over to explore. He made his way past a few rocks and more grass and just kept traveling. He tried to be brave just like Germaine but he knew he wasn't doing a very good job.

He decided to get on top of a rock and look over the area he was about to cross. He struggled to get to the top but realized once he got there that he had about a days-worth of travel ahead of him. Threatened by the long travel he noticed little tiny bugs that were eating the grass and some grass hoppers every now and then would cross his path, but the journey was not unpleasant in any way.

He discovers all kinds of bugs. He watches them eat the grass.

His thoughts were interrupted as he noticed all the bugs had disappeared and the sound of the dirt being slid around was the only thing he could hear. He peered around the corner and realized that he was about to be lunch again. He saw a scorpion staring him right in the face, and freaked. He started to run and then realized the scorpion was right there in front of him again.

He started to panic and tried to hide behind blades of grass but that was no use because he was right back face to face with the scorpion again. Felix looked around to see where he could go and he could not see any place that looked like it would be safe from that monster that was on his path. So Felix did a brave thing he jumped on the scorpions head and ran all the way down its body to the tail.

🙂 *Before he knows it he runs into a scorpion. The scorpion does not let him get away. The scorpion traps Felix and does not let him run.*

He took a flying leap to get on the other side of a rock that was behind the scorpion and barely made it. The scorpion had no idea where he went. His evil and frightening eyes looked from one side to the other but did he not see Felix.

Felix felt something pulling on his leg from under the rock. He jumped back and wondered what was it? He felt the pull on his leg again so he looked down and he saw the leg of what looked like a beetle coming out of the ground. He tried to see what the leg was attached to but he was unable to do so. He started to pull on it. To his surprise the more he pulled the more of the leg he could see and before he knew it a beetle came out of the ground.

Felix runs over the scorpion's body and hides behind a rock. He stumbles upon a leg in the ground so he pulls it. Out comes another very different looking bug.

This beetle was very different. It had a reddish hard covering on it and it had the biggest eyes with the longest eyelashes. Felix was so surprised by this discovery that he was speechless and could not move. He just kept looking at the pretty beetle as it was dusting the dirt off.

He told her that he was running from the scorpion and he accidently came across her. She told him that she too had been hiding from the scorpion for a while and she explained to Felix that she had a sister but the scorpion got her. She'd been all by herself since then and she was trying to escape but every time the scorpion would find her. Felix asked the beetle what her name was and she told him her name was Zailana. He paused, smiled and told her his name.

The beetle is a pretty beetle and her name is Zailana. Felix is speechless. He explained that he was running from the scorpion.

Felix was so sure the scorpion would return so he told her that he had to be on his way. She understood. She then told him that he would not find anything in the direction he was going. Felix thanked her for the advice but decided to continue on despite what she said.

Before he knew it a bunch of rats started to come towards him and once again he knew he was lunch. He began to run and noticed a tiny hole in the ground. It did not look like much but it was his only choice. He took whatever energy he had left, closed his eyes and clinched his fists and took a dive for it.

He barely made it in the hole as the rats passed by. They figured he had gotten away so they journeyed to another area. He was shaking trying to catch his breath when not soon after that Zailana appeared with the "I told you so" look on her face. Breathing heavily and shaking like a leaf on a tree on a windy day he sat down. She gave him leaves she gathered and she sat down beside him, and told him she learned the hard way and showed him the paths that were safe to travel.

She explains that the scorpion ate her sister and warns him about the dangers. He ignores her warning and starts walking away. Shortly after that he is discovered by some hungry rats and barely finds the nearest hole to jump in to.

He looked at all the options and decided on the one that looked the least complicated. As Zailana wished him luck he started to walk in the opposite direction. Felix started walking and realized it was nice having someone around to talk to. He turned around and called to her. She stopped and turned around with a smile.

As they walked in silence, Felix did not know what to say and Zailana was waiting for him to say something. Then suddenly, Zailana grabbed Felix abruptly and told him to stop and be quiet. She heard something that sounded like it was getting closer. It was a squeaky noise and it would stop from time to time but then it would start up again.

🙂 *Shaking like a leaf he is relieved that he was not lunch for some rats, then Felix shyly looked at Zialana and before he could say anything she started walking with him.*

Felix looked at Zailana while she stayed still listening to the noise. Then the dust started to fly and the ground was moving a little.

Felix looked up and saw a big red metal thing, he did not know what it was but it was huge. Attached to the big red metal thing was a little boy that was picking up stuff from the ground like rocks, leaves, and sticks. The little boy could not see Zailana and Felix. Suddenly Felix got an idea if they got on the red metal thing they would get a free ride across the yard. He told Zailana his idea and she agreed. Felix grabbed a leaf and both the bugs hid underneath it. The little boy discovered the leaf and went to pick it up. When he grabbed it, they held on tight.

They both discover a wagon being pulled by a boy. Felix makes the suggestion to use the wagon for a ride. Zailana agrees and with much struggle gets on the wagon.

They were enjoying their nice relaxing ride so much that they both fell asleep. The little boy walked up on to a cemented area that had water flowing in it. He started taking the stuff out of the wagon when Felix and Zailana woke up. Felix grabbed on the leaf and secured his hold on Zailana when the little boy lifted the leaf they were securely holding on. The water was flowing quickly and the cement was getting splashed by it.

Felix and Zailana were left on the cement but were happy because they were close to water. They started to walk and look around. Felix turned around and Zailana was gone. He called out to her but she did not answer.

🙂 *They travel for some time and wonder where they are going. They are both so relaxed that they both take a little nap. The little boy unloads the wagon. The beetles are left on the ground.*

Then out of the corner of his eye Felix saw Zailana being dragged away by a much bigger beetle then himself. The huge beetle landed in the water and started to swim. The large beetle was so fast Felix lost sight of him. Felix grabbed on to a branch that was hanging from the cement and started to climb down it towards the water. Felix could feel the water splashing on his face and could not see well because of it. Rushing to save Zailana he saw an area that was covered in sticks and branches and he jumped with all his might. As he landed he had to pull himself out of the water just to stay on the rubbish. He looked around for Zailana and the beast that took her but he could not find them.

They want to see the beautiful place they were brought to. Zailana gets pulled away from them by a bigger beetle. Felix knows he has to find her.

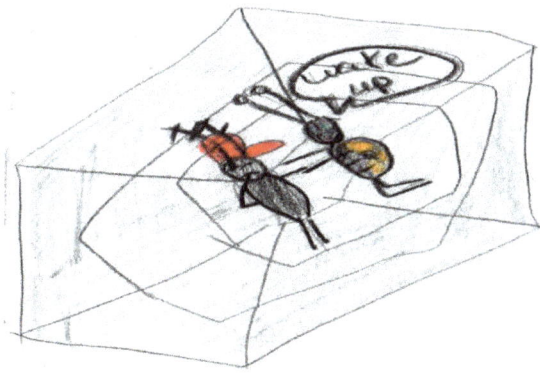

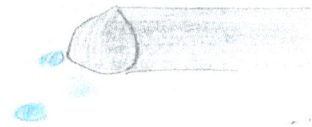

The water was still flowing quickly but the top of the tunnel was dry and he knew he could climb it. He started to climb when he ran into a web. He thought for sure he was stuck and that there was no way to get out. He could not move his legs and he was getting more tangled up as he would try to break free. Suddenly, the water splashed the web and freed him. He crawled into a hole that was on the top of the tunnel. He came upon a grey beetle that was trapped. He tried to help free him but he also did not want to get stuck. Felix knew that water would help and he told the beetle he would be back to save him. He was thinking about that poor beetle and how he was going to free him when he came upon a familiar face. It looked like Germaine. He took a second look and realized that it was Germaine. Germaine's eyes were closed and he could not move. Germaine was also trapped in the web.

Then he heard more talking and there were several other beetles that he walked by that were trapped. Felix was sure he was going to get trapped and then he saw his mother and father were there and stuck in the web also. By the look of them he knew that they were sick and he had to do something.

He discovers a tunnel and travels through it. He finds many beetles wrapped up in web and tries to help them. He eventually finds Germaine with very little strength and helps him.

Felix had to have a plan, he had to help his family but he could not do it alone. He went back to find Germaine and he tried to wake him up. He knew that Germaine would be the one to help him if he could. He kept shaking Germaine and telling him that he was Felix and he was there to save him. Germaine slowly opened his eyes and Felix could tell he was weak by the way he looked at him.

Germaine just looked at Felix and did not move. Felix got an idea and he ran back down the tunnel that was full of bugs and he grabbed a leaf and made a little bowl shape out of it. He waited for the water to splash up the tunnel again and hoped several droplets would make it on the leaf. Felix grabbed the leaf and started to run. He ran so fast that he almost passed by Germaine. By the time he got to him he had a few droplets of water left. He gave it to Germaine and once he finished the droplets of water Felix tore up the leaf and fed it to him.

He finds his family and goes back to get Germaine. Germaine regains his strength. Felix explains to Germaine about Zailana and they both go to help her.

Germaine regained his strength but he was still stuck in the web. Felix remembered that the water had helped him so he ran back down the tunnel to collect more water. He saw the water coming up again and held out the leaf but this time the water grabbed Felix and threw him back in the stream. Felix was struggling to stay above water and swim to safety. He had already swallowed so much water that he could not swim much longer. He grabbed on to a leaf that was sitting on the edge of the cement but the leaf just got carried with the water. He was ready to give up and let the water swallow him when a small beaver carrying a log across the tunnel trapped the water with the log and Felix floated on to the log. He did not wait to see if he was going to be eaten so he picked up his little legs and with the limited strength he had left made a run for it.

Once Felix got back with a mouth full of water he spit it out at Germaine and tried his best to free him. Once freed, Germaine was back to normal and ready to fight.

🙂 *Felix goes to get more water and almost drowns. A beaver drops a log in the way and slows down the flow of the water. Thankful Felix is able to escape.*

Felix knew that Germaine would lead the way from then on. Then Felix remembered that he had not found Zailana yet. He explained to Germaine that there was one more beetle that he had to save. Germaine understood and they both went to look for her.

They got to an opening in the tunnel and decided to go down it. There they found Zailana being tortured by the humongous beetle that had grabbed her. She looked scared and helpless. Germaine looked over the situation and thought quickly. He told Felix to climb the other side of the tunnel and collect some dirt on a leaf. Felix did what Germaine asked him to do.

When he returns, the big monster beetle is torturing Zailana. Germaine and Felix have a plan.

While the large beetle was torturing Zailana, he grabbed on to the spider that was beside him and told him to make a web. He was going to get her tangled in the web just like he had with everyone else. Germaine made a noise by throwing a pebble against the cement wall to distract the beetle. When the beetle turned, they both lifted the leaf with dirt on it with all their might and threw it at the beetle. The beetle could not see because the dirt had gotten in its eyes and the spider got free from its grip. Immediately, Germaine grabbed Zailana and pulled her to the other side along with Felix. When Zailana turned around she saw that the spider was aiming to shoot its web right at them. She jumped higher than she had ever jumped before and grabbed on to the spider so it could not hurt her friends. She pulled with all her might to make the spider stop but the spider weaved its web around the humongous beetle. Zailana, Felix, and Germaine were relieved and over joyed.

They stall the monster beetle by throwing dirt in its eyes. They all escape from the monster.

The spider looked at them and told them her name was Lari. The beetle had been using her to trap all the smaller bugs so he could use them as bait to catch his prey. He was probably the biggest beetle in the world and he did not eat leaves or bushes he ate snails, fish, baby turtles and other aquatic animals, but now he was trapped and he could never hurt them again.

Felix found his family and Germaine finally found his father. After regaining his strength, they were thankful and happy to see them. Zailana, Germaine, and Felix looked at each other. They didn't say it but they knew they sure made a good team. Germaine and Felix both turned to Zailana and gave her a thumbs up.

They are all free from the monster beetle. Germaine and Felix look at each other then look at Zailana and give her the thumbs up! They do not have to say anything they all just know they made a great team.

www.ingramcontent.com/pod-product-compliance
Lightning Source LLC
Chambersburg PA
CBHW062022090426

42811CB00005B/923